Pet Tails

Heartwarming Photos and Stories of Real Pets

Photos and Stories by Borders Customers
Compiled by Shelley O'Hara
with Assistance from Meagan Burger

BORDERS®

This book is dedicated to pet parents everywhere.

For general information on our other products and services or to obtain technical support please contact our Customer Care Department within the U.S. at (800) 762-2974, outside the U.S. at (317) 572-3993 or fax (317) 572-4002.

Wiley also publishes its books in a variety of electronic formats. Some content that appears in print may not be available in electronic books. For more information about Wiley products, please visit our web site at www.wiley.com.

ISBN-13 978-0-470-03764-5

ISBN-10 0-470-03764-4

Printed in the United States of America

10   9   8   7   6   5   4   3   2   1

Book design by Erin Zeltner
Cover design by José Almaguar
Book production by Wiley Publishing, Inc. Composition Services

Table of Contents

Introduction

To start, thank you to the many, many pet owners who responded to our call for photos of your pets. When we put up the BordersPetProject.com site, we wondered whether we would receive enough submissions to make a book. In retrospect, we should have known better! This became more clear as we began

poring through the thousands of photos we received in the short two months the site accepted them; you sent in fantastic photos and stories, each documenting your special relationship with your pet. Each photo and story was lovingly reviewed by several editors (all pet lovers, naturally). We read stories of how pets saved you or your child's life; eased your grief over the loss of a loved one; cheered you up during dark days; helped you get through a divorce or over a broken heart; aided your or another's recovery from cancer, depression, or some other illness or disability; celebrated with you during a windfall; and just generally loved you unconditionally, whole-heartedly, and without reservation, as we all deserve to be loved. We heard tales of abandoned pets rescued, and a clear message was, "I'm not sure if I rescued the pet, or he rescued me." And personalities! We know each of your pets is unique, heroic, hilarious, and well loved. What a treat it was to get to know these pets that have so enriched your lives.

Thanks to you, this book contains a wonderful cross-section of all the photos, stories, poems, and homages to your pets. We've included not only dogs and cats, but a rooster, a hedgehog, a goat, a sugar glider, lots of winged friends, and other furry and feathered family members too numerous to mention. You'll see pets being regal, heroic, silly, snuggly, caring, aloof, and everything in between.

It was a rewarding job reviewing all of the submissions, and the overwhelming love you have for your pets was resounding, uplifting, and inspiring. We hope you find stories and pictures here that illustrate this love. Tonight be sure to give your pet an extra hug, pat on the head, or special treat, and together enjoy this celebration of all that pets bring to our lives.

My Best Friend

Pets come into peoples' lives in lots of ways. Some are abandoned and then rescued by loving pet parents. Some are adopted from local pet shelters. Some are bred by enthusiasts who love and honor the breed. Sometimes serendipity takes a hand and a pet parent not even looking for a new friend comes face-to-face with the perfect pet. There's something about that initial meeting, where with one look, you know that you and your pet belong together. So many pet parents, in fact, have claimed that they never actually picked their pet, but the pet picked them!

Meeting your friend for the first time is delightful, often magical. With that first look, you're bonded for life. It's here that you get a glimpse of your pet's personality and the joy to come. As you and your pet grow, you capture and remember that exact moment when your buddy stole your heart. Warm memories and loving companionship are only a few of the things you will share. Whether it's a dog, a cat, a turtle, an iguana, a goat, a fish, or another animal, each person seems to find the perfect friend.

Peering out from his round glass bowl, Bruiser, a betta, always watches his pet parent Jennifer do the dishes. Jennifer says of Bruiser, who was a gift from her boyfriend, "Kitchen chores just wouldn't be the same without him!"

Photo by Jennifer Segner

Erica calls this picture "Portrait of a Hedgehog." She bought her hedgehog, Enzo, from a breeder; Enzo likes to rearrange his furniture and patter across the floor as if he's on a super-secret mission. Here he's playing with an old clam can.

Photo by Erica Booth

Johnny got to fulfill his childhood dream of owning a pet when he received Kimmi from his aunt. He's especially attached to Kimmi because he had made earlier plans to get a puppy, but then the house where the puppy lived was robbed, and the burglar took that particular puppy. In hindsight, he says, without the burglary, he wouldn't have Kimmi, who is now part of the family.

Photo by Johnny Vy

This gentle and affectionate rat named Charlie likes to take walks on his pet parent's shoulder.

Photo by Lauren Browne

Raleigh, a Jack Russell Terrier, is described by her pet parent as "Mrs. Personality." Here she's standing on landscape timbers, watching cars drive by.

Photo by Jessica Skaggs

Glen drove 4 hours from Dallas to south Texas to pick up his "fantaBULLus" English Bulldog, Sir Otis. He says that it's amazing how much fun a silly, slobbery 80-pound bundle of fur can bring.

Photo by Glen Johnson

Gracie and Dancer are described by their pet parent as spirited, beautiful, and trusting.

Photo by Kellie Bambach

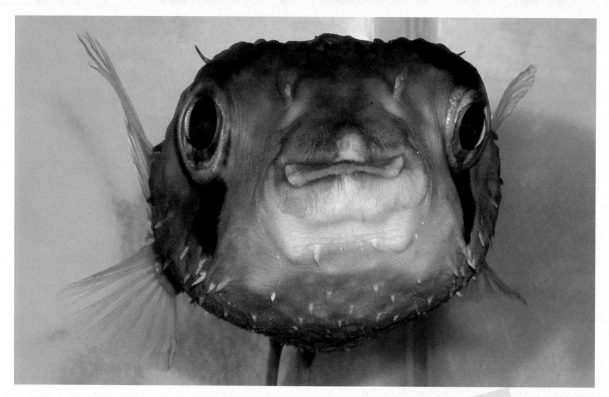

Puffy, the so-called Shrimp Slayer, gets excited when her pet parent opens the freezer (because that's where her shrimp is kept!). She also greets visitors who lift the lid of the tank by spitting at them—sometimes to a distance of 4 feet.

Photo by Bonnie Miller

Callie was found hiding in a garage after a thunderstorm. The garage owners were going to take her to the SPCA, but Janet intervened and took the dog. She had Callie checked at the vet for an owner ID microchip and also contacted several agencies to try to find the owner. When no one appeared, Callie became a beloved member of Janet's family.

Photo by Janet Murray

Kelly describes her Django as a big dog who just happens to be little. In this picture, he shows that he knows that he's going to Granny's, where he can have a snack.

Photo by Kelly Kievit

This is one of the first baby pictures of Lexie, no bigger than a blade of grass. Here she's stopping at a rest stop on her way home from the breeder with her new pet parents.

Photo by Darcell Sutka

Boyfriend, a White-Crested Black Polish rooster, got his name because he is quite the ladies' man. Despite his reputation, he is always a gentleman, letting his hens eat first and dancing and strutting around to entertain his special girl, Beep.

Photo by Cheri Skipp

Sydney loved her first outing in the snow so much that her pet parent had a hard time getting her to come back inside.

Photo by Kipp Downey

A New Lease on Life for Coton de Tulear Dogs

Robert Jay Russell discovered Coton de Tulear dogs while studying on the island of Madagascar and was immediately smitten by the breed's intelligent, loving nature. He vowed to bring the breed to the United States. Starting in the late 1970s, he sent a small group of the dogs to the United States, and his parents picked them up at the airport and cared for them until he completed his studies and returned.

While caring for the dogs, his parents also became enamored with them, and they joined their son in his quest to carefully breed the dogs and establish a club to protect the breed from extinction, exploitation, and genetic harm. In fact, Robert's parents devoted the rest of their lives to the dogs. After Robert's father passed away, his mother developed Alzheimer's disease, and now she lives in a home devoted to the care of people with this disease.

In this photo, Robert's mother, who helped save this dog breed from extinction, pets and talks to Girigirika, a Coton de Tulear puppy. Her son writes that the dog fondly reminds his mother of days feeding and playing with the puppies, and in doing so, helps his mother remember the emotion love.

Photo and story by
Robert Jay Russell, Ph.D.

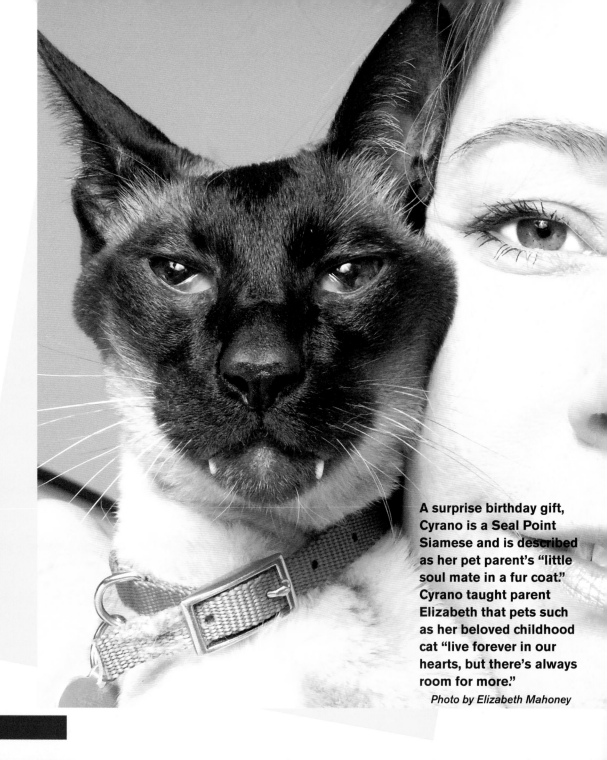

A surprise birthday gift, Cyrano is a Seal Point Siamese and is described as her pet parent's "little soul mate in a fur coat." Cyrano taught parent Elizabeth that pets such as her beloved childhood cat "live forever in our hearts, but there's always room for more."

Photo by Elizabeth Mahoney

A neighbor's dog found Tank in an azalea bed; Tank was later given to James, who's known as "Ranger Jim" in the neighborhood. Tank likes to bask in the warm sun atop the back of his cast-resin toad pal.

Photo by James Minor

Cocoa, a 4-pound puppy, grew into a 90-pound dog. Her pet parents aren't sure of her breed but get lots of questions. Is she a bear cub? Is she part wolf? Cocoa adapted well when her parents expanded their family to include a child. Cocoa welcomed the new baby by placing one of her treats under the bassinet.

Photo by Maria Buchert

This Maltese named Misha once logged on to her pet parent's instant messaging account—perhaps trying to order a new diamond collar!

Photo by Sandra Rouse

Lindsey found her pet goat Petunia through an ad in the paper. This Alpine Dairy goat eats anything and everything.

Photo by Lindsey Christ

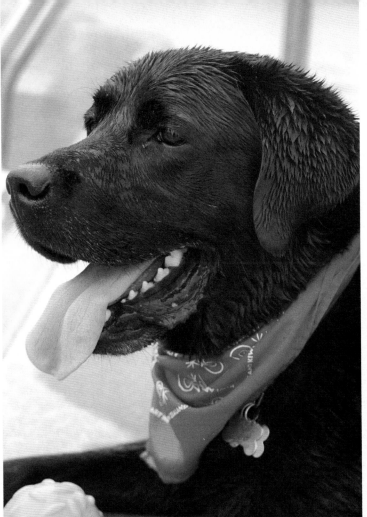

Angus was adopted from a shelter in Rochester, New York, and helped her pet parents deal with the painful loss of two of their much-loved pets. When the parents received an e-mail with photos attached, they said, "Hold that dog!" When they picked up Angus, it was "love at first lick."

Photo by Martha Armstrong

Pet parent Robin rescued Molly from a dog shelter and purchased Ralph from a pet store. Both hold a special place in her heart.

Photo by Robin Borim

This picture of Riley MacFluff was taken the day after his pet parent, Joy, brought him home from the breeder; he was exploring the deck and stuck his head through the bars to get a better look at Joy.

Photo by Joy Dal Santo

Little Pouka was only three weeks old when this adorable photo was taken.

Photo by Carrie Stoyak

Phoebe Bouffet, a Yorkshire Terrier, joined her family when another family decided she didn't fit with their other dogs. Although her siblings (the pet parents' other Yorkies) snubbed her, she eventually won them over.

Photo by Lisa Stanton

Initially, Bean was on loan to see whether it was true that chinchillas are hypo-allergenic. Luckily for both Bean and his pet parent, Allison, he was, and he's been living with Allison since.
Photo by Allison Elsby

When Andrew and his wife visited Rocket Dog Rescue, they were introduced to Otis, who had been abandoned at the age of 5 weeks. Otis climbed into Andrew's lap and fell fast asleep, and Andrew knew immediately that Otis was their new four-legged family member.

Photo by Andrew Freeman

This loyal, loving, and cuddly Cavalier King Charles Spaniel is named Spenser Kensington. He is shown here relaxing after a hard day of playing.

Photo by Daniel Ingram

Wendy Kaplan's cat Butterscotch gave birth to Callie, shown here sipping milk, underneath the porch.

Photo by Wendy Kaplan

Chewie arrived at his pet parent's town via an airplane from Canada. He's very popular in the neighborhood and loves the snow. He's often seen hopping around as if he's half puppy and half bunny.

Photo by Suzanne Drazba

Butch Mwba turned up at his pet parents' yard during their service as Peace Corps volunteers in Kenya. It took some finagling to get him from Africa to his new home. The adventure included both a trip to the vet in Nairobi and an export certificate, but now he's the happiest dog ever.

Photo by JoAnna Haugen

When Danica visited her boyfriend, she found a little water and food dish and a crate with a note that said "Marry me? Or you can't have what's inside." She said yes, and now Maya, the surprise inside the crate, is one of two loves of her life.

Photo by Danica Stachowski

For her 13th birthday, Suzanne got what she wanted—an iguana, Iggy—from her aunt and uncle. Here he is, basking in the sunshine.

Photo by Suzanne Bacon

Lauren raises rabbits for the American Rabbit Breeders Association and shows them on a national level. Bambi, shown here, was from the first litter she raised. Now retired, Bambi shares a cardboard house with his mother, Blondi.

Photo by Lauren Nicholas

Luckily for Heather's husband, he saw a German Shepherd Dog and told the owner how much his wife would love the dog. The mother of the dog had just had puppies, and they snagged the last one, Roscoe.

Photo by Heather Stelitano

Almost 18 years ago, Lola was given to her pet parent, Sara Bullock, by Sara's cousins; Lola's hobbies include swimming among the Greek ruins at the bottom of her tank, sunbathing, and being hand-fed.

Photo by Sara Bullock

Once neglected, Willie came strolling up Rebecca's driveway and into her life at a particularly trying time, after the death of her father. Rebecca has always felt that her dad sent Willie to her to let her know that he's still with her.

Photo by Rebecca Smallman

Onyx was with pet parent Jeff for 17 years! Among her brothers and sisters, Onyx was the most eager to fetch and wrestle, so she's the dog Jeff picked from the litter of eight.

Photo by Jeff Tisman

Beatrix was hit by a car and rescued and nursed back to health by a friend. Because the friend had too many pets of her own, Beatrix came to live with Kelly, and they've been great pals since.

Photo by Kelly Blaine

Monica's husband was initially hesitant to bring a dog into their home. But once he met Foster at a ranch in Montana, he fell in love. Foster is now an integral part of the family.

Photo by Monica Dupre

Take It Easy

2

Pets know how to kick back and relax, and they'll do it just about anywhere—in your bed, on the couch, under the covers, in the shade. There's something satisfying about seeing your pet just taking it easy, whether it's in the house, on a trip, with a buddy, or all alone. They're just so darn cute and so innocent! And they are not up to trouble at that moment.

Your pet can be a reminder to not be on the go all the time, to enjoy some rest and relaxation, to slow down or cuddle up. So the next time your four-legged or feathered friend is sprawled on the sofa or snoozing on your favorite cashmere sweater, use it as a reminder to take some time for yourself!

When a friend found Russell abandoned at a gas station, she asked Donna to take care of the dog just until a new home could be found. Donna, however, decided to keep Russell, and he has found that he can finally relax and be at peace in his new home.

Photo by Donna Lamberth

Zeus, a Doberman Pinscher, was adopted from the local pound, and Elmo, a Boston Terrier, came from a breeder. Here they are relaxing in the sunshine on a nice afternoon.

Photo by Lisa Vitale

Is Noddy yawning here or sticking out his tongue at one of his siblings, Fatboy or Lily? His pet parent found this abandoned dog behind a gas station and welcomed him to the family, where he's clearly made himself at home.

Photo by Sonya Wilkinson

Company, who loves lounging next to pet parent Adele's keyboard, was found 18 years ago, abandoned on the steps of a church. Adele took him in and has spent every moment since enjoying her housemate, dinner companion, and "company."

Photo by Adele Azar-Rucquoi

Wouldn't we all love such plush bedding and snuggling pleasure? Mocha, a Pug, keeps an eye on her pet parents as they get ready in the morning.

Photo by J.R. and Erika Obrecht

Soupcon was a Father's Day present for pet parent Terri's husband. This photo shows the typically rambunctious and energetic Labrador enjoying a quiet moment.

Photo by Terri Garneau

After a day at the beach, Seven dug a hole to hide in the shade. Seven is a lucky pooch who was adopted into his family from a local animal shelter.

Photo by Jeff Tomsik

Second Chance
for Autumn

Her pet parent, Wendy, found Autumn abandoned behind a gas station in Los Angeles, California; she was cold and hungry and needed help. Wendy bought her cat food and scratched her back, and then she cried because she lived in Atlanta, Georgia, and didn't know how to take the cat with her.

Autumn was eventually picked up and taken to an animal shelter. There she was cleaned up, fed, and placed in a warm bed. She waited patiently for a parent to adopt her. Meanwhile, back in Atlanta, Wendy regretted her decision to leave the cat and worried. She asked her companion to find the cat, and he started searching for the cat via the Internet. He found her at the shelter and made a special trip to pick up Autumn. He called Wendy in Atlanta, and she flew out to pick up her new cat. Wendy had only been off the airplane for a few minutes before Autumn was in her arms, being kissed and hugged.

Autumn then flew back to Atlanta with Wendy. She was a good cat the entire flight, sleeping most of the time. She didn't even have to use the litter box. In this picture, she's taking a break from her pet carrier on a layover in San Diego, California.

At her new home in Atlanta, Autumn has reveled in the love and happiness of her newfound family.

B24

Photo and story by Wendy Gardiner

Here Tukis is taking a much-needed break on the couch after being kissed on her nose repeatedly by pet parent Kristaq's young daughter.

Photo by Kristaq Reinhardt

After a long afternoon, trying to get a good Christmas picture, pet parent Jessi got lucky when Bailey and Boscoe became exhausted and fell sound asleep. Jessi then captured the perfect picture of them snoring side by side.

Photo by Jessi Ankeles

Simba gave up the top spot for Stitch on the bathroom towel rack. Pet parent Alyssa finally moved the rack after growing tired of drying off with cat hair!

Photo by Alyssa Peters

These Boxers were rescued from the Los Angeles Boxer Rescue. Cloud was picked up first, and then pet parent Carmen got a call about Cloud's brother, Cotton. Carmen couldn't bear to keep the boys apart, and the two brothers have remained the best of friends.

Photo by Carmen Grey

Alex, a Golden Retriever, shows the effects of too much partying.
Photo by Julie Caouette

Tio, a Border Collie, was adopted by pet parent Mim after spending time in an abusive family. Through love and nurturing, he began to trust and interact with his new family. Now Tio loves playing with others, like Mim's nephew Ryan and his dog Jasmine.
Photo by Mim Schreck

Cats and dogs enemies? Not these two. When Ojo wasn't feeling well, Squirty gave Ojo a much-needed hug, and they curled up for a long nap together in the sun.

Photo by Laurie Herbst

Ruby Lou likes to nap on her favorite chair, which gets flooded with afternoon sun. This photo was taken just as she was about to drift off.

Photo by Dawn Norris

Buster and Baron, Dachshund brothers and best friends, were adopted together because the adopting family couldn't bear to part the siblings.

Photo by Kay Stevenson

Suca sleeps with her tongue out, and when she's dreaming, her whiskers often twitch.

Photo by Lindsay Guaman

The Great Outdoors

3

Pets enjoy playing outside, whether they're fetching a stick, playing Frisbee, jumping in a lake, rolling in leaves, romping in snow, running on a beach, or kicking back on a boat. They know how to enjoy nature, and they know how to make the best of a beautiful day—even if they sometimes get into trouble for digging holes in your yard or eating your prized flowers.

The next time you're outside with your pet, look closely. You'll see the innate pleasure they take in enjoying their surroundings. Chances are you'll agree that nothing can compete with the combination of a great day, the open air, and your best friend.

Indulge yourself and your pet. There's no finer place to bond than in the great outdoors.

Here's a perfect example of stopping to smell the flowers. In fact, Lexus, a Pug, even tried to lick this flower!

Photo by Mandy Eby

Capri, a Standard Poodle, loves to pose! Here she's showing off her Halloween handkerchief, which coordinates perfectly with the fall leaves.

Photo by Melissa Yost

When Batman was diagnosed with cancer, his pet parent decided to do something special with him every day. On the day this picture was snapped, they were on their way to the beach, and Batman paused for a few moments of reflection.

Photo by Barbara Robertson

When a giant snapping turtle tried to settle into the front garden of the Towles' home, Lisa sent both her dogs to negotiate an eviction. Imbali, the Rhodesian Ridgeback pictured here, gently moved in on the turtle, while Lisa's other dog, a Jack Russell Terrier named Indy, paced, quivered, yapped, and taunted the turtle.

Photo by Lisa Towle

Toodie is a search-and-rescue dog, and in her work, she isn't hesitant to leap over logs, hop through tall grass, and navigate swamps and woods. Underneath, though, she's a pretty lady, as shown in this picture in front of a waterfall at Rickett's Glen State Park.

Photo by Deb Lusby

Maggie, a boxer, loves playing in the fall leaves.

Photo by Michelle Wittmer

Casey was adopted from the Humane Society, and his pet parent penned this short poem in his honor:

There once was a Husky named Casey
Whose previous owners were hasty
He found a good home
From which he won't roam
As long as the treats are tasty.

Photo by Margaret Rushton

Rucker Roo was rescued on the side of a highway when he was only 8 weeks old. He was matched with his new family, and he often comes to work with his pet parent at the Marin Humane Society.

Photo by Kim Snyder

Kodiak, a Siberian Husky, has a talent for getting lost; he's been lost in Oklahoma, Florida, and on a camping trip in Colorado. On the camping trip, Kodiak's pet parents finally abandoned the search and drove home. Distraught at losing Kodiak, however, one of the parents drove the 250 miles back to the camp site, where a tired Kodiak was waiting by the site's fire pit.

Photo by Rebecca Kane

Baby and Sand are shown here with a friend fetching a stick in the Chesapeake Bay. It's Sand's first swim, but as you can guess, it won't be his last!

Photo by Leandra Aubry

"Joy"dale on the Farm

Joydale "Sparky" Sparklerlas, a registered Morgan mare, came into Elizabeth's life when Elizabeth was 13 and Sparky was 10. Elizabeth first saw Sparky chained to the wall in a straight stall with no bedding. There were no signs of food, and Sparky had only brown water from a frozen pond to drink. Elizabeth knew immediately that she had to save this horse!

Sparky's life had been very unstable; Elizabeth was Sparky's 11th owner in 10 years. The horse had been deserted at a horse farm, denied food for being sensitive to train, and repeatedly thrown to the ground because she allegedly reared. When Elizabeth took over Sparky's care, she started slowly and built trust. At first, Sparky wouldn't even let Elizabeth brush her. Using patience and understanding, Elizabeth helped Sparky progress from a scared, unruly horse to a well-trained athlete. Sparky has been shown in open shows, dressage, hunter paces, and combined training. As a team, Elizabeth and Sparky have won more than 50 ribbons, many first and second places.

At 19, Sparky retired from jumping and became a driving horse. In fact, she won her last combined driving event in 2005. (This picture is from that event.) Elizabeth recounts, "Showing her has been one of the highlights of my life, but I cherish the quiet times, too. I love to look out my kitchen window and see her in her pasture." Sparky will spend the rest of her days trail riding, getting her coat brushed, and enjoying her farm and family.

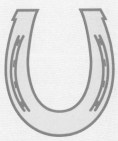

Boomer loves to travel; here he's on his first vacation to Estes Park, Colorado. He especially liked looking at the view from Rainbow Curve, a trail road in Rocky Mountain National Park.

Photo by Ryan Frownfelter

Boulder was rescued by a group of New Yorkers who were vacationing in Boulder, Colorado. They found him running loose on a street. After attempting to locate his original family, his current parents adopted him. He now splits his time between living in Colorado and living in Florida.

Photo by Merald Conn

Pet parent Mindy describes Muffin, a Cocker Spaniel/Lhaso Apso mix, as mellow and angelic and a constant provider of unconditional love.

Photo by Mindy Gaebel

Gracie was rescued by a member of Furry Friends Rescue from Los Banos Animal Shelter in California; she's described as sweet, quiet, and well-behaved, just as she appears here.

Photo by Emily Verna

Menaka was abandoned, but her luck changed when Nicole, who lived on the same street where Menaka was abandoned, found and adopted her.

Photo by Nicole Hopkins

On their first wedding anniversary, the Pacellis went to a breeder and picked out Toby Reese, their Pembroke Welsh Corgi. This picture shows Toby's first trip to the beach.

Photo by Stephanie Pacelli

**Maria, in her little life vest, enjoys a day on the
water during a camping trip to Lake McConaughy
in Nebraska.**
Photo by Melissa Vette

Murphy was adopted the high-tech way: He was listed online, where pet parent Wendi found and fell in love with him.

Photo by Wendi Steadham

On Midas's first trip to the mountains of North Carolina, he enjoyed himself as much as Joe, his pet parent!

Photo by Joe Cardo

When Molly's big brown eyes locked onto Linda's at a local animal shelter, that was it! Linda knew she had to take Molly home. Molly is most likely a survivor of the F5 tornado that recently ravaged central Oklahoma. These days, everything's coming up pansies for Molly.

Photo by Linda Bosteels

Beth and her husband adopted Smiley, a greyhound, and were so thrilled that they added Peanut, another greyhound, to the family.

Photo by Beth Wade

Duke and his pet parent love playing together. Just look at the expression on Duke's face!

Photo by Jessie Schwartz-Land

Lady Luck was on Bryan's side when he spotted Leika at the Chicagoland German Shepherd Pet Rescue. Because someone else also wanted to adopt Leika, the two potential adopters settled the matter with a coin toss, which Bryan won.

Photo by Bryan Keadle

Remington, a rescued dog, has special roles, including being an unconditional love-giver, a protector, a personal exercise director, a dishwasher, an interior decorator, and a backseat driver.

Photo by Virginia Crowell

On his airplane trip to his new home, Nikolai enjoyed quite an adventure. On his boarding pass, he was flagged for additional security clearance and was patted down and checked by a security agent (male, of course). Nikolai was pleased with the extra attention, and you can see that attitude in his purposeful, confident stride as he explores his new home in this photo.

Photo by Jean Mansen

Teddy Baer, a Schipperke, was a surprise Christmas gift for Terry, his pet parent. Teddy loves hiking in the snow on the beaches at Lake Tahoe, California.

Photo by Terry Turner-Baade

Meep's pet parents found her living under their house and welcomed her into the family. Meep has since moved into the house and made herself right at home.

Photo by Ami Flori

Oscar lives on a farm, and despite his small size, his pet parent claims he acts and performs his duties like a perfect farm dog.

Photo by Anya Lafreniere

Austin not only enjoys playing in the snow, he also likes to eat the snowflakes.
Photo by Paul Pasquariello

Zarco took pleasure in the days following a record snow fall, sprinting across the snow, tunneling through snow mounds, and then taking a rest.
Photo by Nelson Grisales-Gutierrez

Looking Good

4

Getting a pet to pose for a camera is no small task. So, if you can catch their sweetness on camera, all the better. Some pets are real hams and love posing—whether they're just hanging out with their buddies or sporting a costume that makes them the life of the party. The hammiest of pets let you pose them in outfits and in different settings; they are the ultimate photo model because they can't talk back! And even if they don't like their picture taken, you can always sneak a few shots catching them napping or at play or sometimes in the midst of trouble.

Some pets love to dress to the nines: tuxedos at weddings, costumes on Halloween, sparkly collars for a night on the town. But whether they're sporting a whole costume, a dashing hat, or simply some attitude and a well-groomed coat, pets know how to look good. Take a look at your pet the next time he thinks you're not looking, and enjoy him at his silly, playful, preening, beautiful best.

Belle is sitting pretty on the porch, taking a break from her duties as guard dog.

Photo by Randy Davey

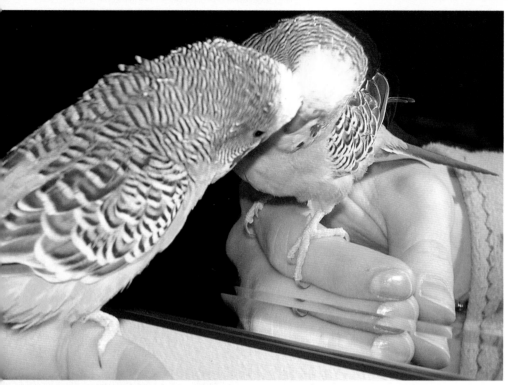

Bert, a parakeet, has a soft white head and feathers as blue as the ocean. He finds he makes quite a conversationalist as he carries on with his own admiring reflection!

Photo by Eric and Karen Landers

This Italian Greyhound, Sophie Doodle, sits pretty as she gets her Christmas picture taken.

Photo by Sue Brandon

Bailey has her own vanity tag. Here she's on the way to an American Cancer Society Dogswalk, which she thoroughly enjoyed. She got to ride in the car, go for a long walk, and make friends with other dogs on the fundraising walk.

Photo by Ellen Wolfson

This is Iris at 10 weeks old, posing patiently with (what else?) a vase of irises.

Photo by Craig Bell

Biker Babe? That's Bonnie. She's logged over 4,000 biking miles. Well, one of her pet parents has, pulling all 45 pounds of her in her little trailer. She's well known and liked in the biking world.

Photo by Sheila Barry

An Abyssinian, Tasha loves the outdoors. She became enthralled with one of her pet parent's many pumpkins and took a moment to pose and get her photo snapped.

Photo by Sherri Dodd

Kiki became a part of her family when she was found living in the bushes on a family walk. Her pet parent lured her with some canned cat food, gently grabbed her, and held on for dear life on the car ride home. Once they got home, though, Kiki quickly realized what a good deal this new house would be: food, a nice warm bed, and lots of love!

Photo by Sandy Garton

This handsome Basset Hound, Heath, looks like a fine old Southern gentleman in his proper hat. His laid-back manner has earned him lots of respect: He has his Canine Good Citizen title, is a registered therapy dog, and has almost completed his AKC breed championship.

Photo by Sandi Bonenberger

Described by her pet parents as a "wonderful old lady who is young at heart," Miss Daisy poses here for a Halloween picture.

Photo by Stephen Kennett

More Than Just a Pretty Face

Jolie was adopted from a Boxer rescue organization. She's done her best to give back to the canine community to show her appreciation, and proudly wears her "I saved a life" scarf every chance she gets.

One of her activities is to donate blood to the Eastern Veterinary Blood Bank. She goes every other month, lies on a comfortable bed, gives blood, and then dines on a gourmet cookie. Each unit of blood she donates can save three other dogs' lives!

In addition to her "blood work," Jolie is also an assistant puppy raiser for Guiding Eyes for the Blind (GEB). Because she's so great with puppies, she mentors potential guide dogs, teaching them, as her pet parent writes, "the delicate art of good dog manners." She tutors her charges in proper house manners, people-greeting etiquette, and dog-greeting etiquette, as well as in how to play fetch and how to respond to obedience commands. So far, she's helped raise five puppies for GEB.

Who would have thought that a discarded pup could end up saving other dogs' lives and helping other dogs go on to help people attain more independent lives? Yes, Jolie is much more than just a pretty face.

Photo and story by Karen Bracken-Penley

Buck is clearly ready for Tampa, Florida's Gasparilla festival, a big weekend celebration with parades, festive beads, and a pirate invasion. He takes on the alias "Buck-aneer" for the festivities.

Photo by Jeanne Jackson

When a stray dog and her 12 pups were rescued from life on the street, amazingly, all the dogs found homes. Three of the siblings, including 2-month-old Houdini, found love with pet parent Emma.

Photo by Emma DeJarnette

Dexter Gordon loves to help out—especially at Halloween, when he dresses up and passes out candy. In addition to his candy duty, he also aids his pet grandpa by letting him know when the phone or doorbell rings, watching game shows with him, and accompanying him on walks.

Photo by Karin Smith

Pete realizes he's about to experience his first bath, but hey, it's not easy remaining the handsome fellow that he is!

Photo by Kellie Kinert

These guinea pigs, Kijafa, Jack, Bailey, and Kahlua, are all gussied up and ready for Valentine's Day.

Photo by Annette Krag-Jensen

This beautiful Papillion, Lulu, likes tummy rubs and chasing squirrels and birds.

Photo by Heather and Tom Cunningham

Emma has won costume contests, has her own Web page, and once helped advertise a company on eBay.

Photo by Melissa Sadecki

Marley, an adoptee from a local Humane Society, stops on a hike and poses, peaking out of an old ranger station.

Photo by Jenni Gibbons

Baby came from an abusive background, but her life turned around when her pet parent flew from Maryland to Ohio to rescue her. Thanks to patience, love, and training, this once insecure, fearful dog is now sweet, playful, affectionate, and obedient.

Photo by Linda Vinh

A Pembroke Welsh Corgi, Titus poses for his Valentine's Day glamor shot.
Photo by Shannon Guthrie

Participating in a Halloween charity walk for New Leash on Life, Pippin good-naturedly dons this hot dog costume and even lets his pet parents snap a picture.

Photo by Nicole Crouch

It's fitting that Benji is dressed in his Santa suit because he was a Christmas gift to his pet parent.

Photo by Heidi Larson

Zeke was destined for his pet parent; he has a spot on his head known as a "haggery" spot, and his pet parent lives off Haggery Road! Here he's dreaming of heading south of the border in his new Mexican sombrero.

Photo by Stacy Cykiert

Jolie is a Toy Poodle who appears every week on the cable TV show *American Visions.*

Photo by Catherine Bene

5

Play Time

Pets can always entertain themselves! Give them a bone, an old plastic soda bottle, or a stuffed toy, and they can amuse themselves for hours. In addition to playing by themselves, though, pets really love spending time with their parents and other animals. Whether it's a game of catch, a jaunt in a convertible, a run on the beach, or a little hide and seek, pets know how to live in the moment and rejoice in the pleasure of playing.

Even if you're feeling like a couch potato, take a couple minutes to play with your pet. Their enthusiasm and joy are contagious, and will instantly brighten your mood. You might even find yourself romping for hours together. So pull out the tennis balls or the cat nip and have some fun. Take a few pictures to capture these moments of carefree play. When you look back, you'll not only be overwhelmed with the love for your pet, but grateful for all the opportunities to savor life.

Here's a perfect example of living the high life. While swimming, Tracy thought, why not let Marley, her Pug, enjoy a dip in the pool. Sure enough, Marley loved floating on his own little raft.

Photo by Tracy Prawdzik

Chester and Emily became friends one day while Emily was eating peanuts on the steps. Chester inched closer and closer, until Emily shared her peanuts, and they've been buddies every since.

Picture by Emily Stone

Toby loves to show his zest for life while running the obstacles of an agility course. He even practices in his pet parents' living room!

Photo by Brian Trede

This photo is from P.J.'s first camping trip. She's riding on a kayak, taking in all the gorgeous scenery at Donner Lake in California.

Photo by Carol Jong

Warm or cold, lake or ocean, morning or night, Lucy can't wait to jump into the water. She's even started participating in competitions, where she's been known to jump over 20 feet!

Photo by Craig Michaels

Playing his favorite game, "Stick," Finnegan shows the energy that pet parent Jen says is boundless. According to Jen, Finnegan would play 24 hours a day if his playmate could only keep up with him.

Photo by Jen Huss

These three are like brothers: B.J. is the big brother and keeps everyone in line; T.J. is the pesky little brother, always trying to get someone to play with him; and J.J. is the good middle brother, mediating when needed.

Photo by Susan Stone

Huey and Strider, both Whippets, are fast! The pair can run up to an amazing 35 miles per hour.

Photo by Katherine Anderson

Pepper, a 2½-year-old cat, finds a great perching ground for springing out and surprising passersby.

Photo by Kristen Harris

Shasta loves tennis balls and the snow. Look at the concentration on that face!

Photo by Mark Evans

A rescued Doberman Pinscher, Luigi enjoys playing fetch with his favorite Fruit Loops ball. He pretends that he can't retrieve it without help, barking his request for assistance until he gets his pet parent to give in and start playing.

Photo by Helen Schwarzmann

Named after a favorite Beatles album, Pepper finds fun in spying through the blinds and lounging on the coffee table.

Photo by Suzanna Thompson

A mixed breed and a stray adopted via the Internet, Peppie must have some hunting and retrieving in her blood because she loves to fish!

Photo by Jackie Ritzko

Ebony's Back in Black (a.k.a., Cody) has completed the Tennessee Walking Horse Versatility Championships, and his picture will be in the Walking Horse Hall of Fame in Tennessee. That lightening bolt on his rump is from one of his many costumes.

Photo by Leslie Anderson

Basil is a Great Dane who likes to play hide-and-seek in his pet parents' yard.
Photo by Jane Reiss

Brando and Diesel, both English Bulldogs, like to roughhouse with each other. Here they are playing with a toy tire.
Photo by Denise Smith

Return Trip for Leroy

Leroy and Missy first met at the airport where she works. He was so cute and friendly, greeting all the passengers and visitors. Missy became enamored with him immediately but wondered where the dog's owners were. She noticed he had a collar and tag, and that meant he had an owner somewhere.

The next day at work, the dog was gone, and Missy figured his owners had picked him up. Yet something made her look around for him anyway, and during her search, she heard whimpering and crying. She followed the cries until she found Leroy stuck in a storm drain. She got him from the drain and called her husband, and together they took Leroy to the vet to tend to his cuts and scrapes. They also placed an ad in the local paper. Time went by, and no one called, so Missy and her husband gladly accepted Leroy into their family.

On the way to work one day, Missy saw a huge sign that read "LOST DOG" and described Leroy perfectly. Heartbroken, she called the owners and explained that she had Leroy but that they had become such good friends that she wondered if she could keep him. Unfortunately for her, the owners wanted him back. Missy returned Leroy to his original home and tried to deal with her sadness.

Two weeks later, something miraculous happened. Leroy's owners called Missy and asked her whether she still wanted him. They said Leroy had been depressed since returning to his original home, and they felt he was best placed back with Missy. Missy eagerly agreed to take back her new friend. Leroy came back "home," where he greets pilots, passengers, and visitors at the airport.

Photo and story by Missy Hatsis

Summit enjoys visits to the coastal areas of Oregon and Northern California. She loves leaping into the surf, walking mountain trails, wading into icy rivers and streams, and, when finally home, plopping down on the sofa.

Photo by James Minor

Star and Stormy trot to their pet parent from across the wide open spaces of a pasture in South Dakota.

Photo by Wendy Olson

A gift from Nicole's husband, Crickett is a sugar glider (an Australian marsupial that's been compared to the flying squirrel). He enjoys exploring the fascinating items in the kitchen.

Photo by Nicole Slough

Spooky, rescued from a shelter, loves to play hide and seek. Pet parent Kathy calls out, "Spooky, where are you?" until she finds— and then tickles—Spooky. Of course, Spooky then expects Kathy to hide, which she does!

Photo by Kathy Dolge

Josie's favorite toy is her soft Frisbee. She grabs it first thing in the morning and expects her pet parent to play then and at least four or five times a day more.

Photo by George Miller

Jennifer's father bought her a Basset Hound, Byron, as a house-warming gift. Their family owns a bicycle shop, and one slow day, they decided to teach Byron to ride a bike.

Photo by Jennifer Bishop

Indy is having a ball, running free in a new pasture.

Photo by Margot Doohan

Angelo, a 9-year-old Scottish Terrier, loves going for rides around town.
Photo by Brian Moss

A West Highland White Terrier, Elvis finds this toy house just perfect for him.
Photo by Sandy Klinkey

Sir Sampson, a Boxer, enjoys
curling up with a good book.
Photo by Melody Kranz

Snack makes the most of
his playground equipment.
He took a break from
running on his wheel
to let his pet parent snap
his picture.
Photo by Amanda Vlasveld

Moby greets his parents with a loving whistle or a nice stretch when they come home. Here he's greeting them with a gift: a newly shed feather.

Photo by Aileen Franzi

Mr. Bojangles (a.k.a., Bobo) loves to go for car rides. When he and his pet parent stop for a rest, he often sits in the open trunk to avoid the very hot pavement.

Photo by Sandra Needham

Pet parent Dana isn't sure what Cayenne likes better: jumping into the lake or shaking off all that water!

Photo by Dana Norvell

One of Buddy's favorite games is to catch tennis balls in midair. His pet parent, Tony, took this photo at the peak of Buddy's jump.

Photo by Tony Garcia

Here's an excerpt from a poem
Brian penned about his Shar-pei
Abbie:

Abbie dog with eyes so wide
Marching into the wind with head
    held high
And when we stare up into the
    blue spring sky
She stays right beside me,
    stride for stride.

Photo by Brian Page

Maisey, a rescue dog from an
anti-cruelty society in Chicago,
wanted to go as a witch this
Halloween!
Photo by Amy Miller

Family & Friends

Pets are an indispensable part of the family. They go on vacations, sleep in human beds, and fill hearts with love. They are also often accepting of new additions, whether another animal or a child, and they can be quite generous in their love and devotion to everyone in the family. And even when there's the inevitable sibling rivalry, things almost always work out in the end.

In addition to their human family, pets have their own family—mothers, brothers, sisters, fathers, cousins—and they enjoy these relationships, also. Add to that their friends, and a pet's world grows even larger. No wonder we adore these open-hearted creatures as much as we do!

Best of Show

Abbie, a Boxer, went to her toy box, and got her favorite baby and offered it to her pet parent's niece when she came for a visit. Luckily, Brenda, the pet parent, had her camera handy to capture this precious moment.

Photo by Brenda Lowery

This neighborhood gang includes Bogey, Marlie, Moxie, Maisy, Daisy, and Zona, all Golden Retrievers and the best of friends.

Photo by Alyssa Wilkinson

Rescued from a local Humane Society, Nala meets a horse for the first time and tries to make friends.
Photo by Stephenie Tanner

Pet parent Tzu-Ying describes Sunny and Greeny as BFF (best friends forever).

Photo by Tzu-Ying Chen

Kristy got her dog, Porter, through the Humane Society; he enjoys hiking with her, her boyfriend, and her boyfriend's dog, Stoli.

Photo by Kristy Berg

Lady Diana loves to dress up for any occasion, especially for her family's Christmas festivities.

Photo by Tom Transou

Pet parent Mandy brings her rabbits Mr. Bella and Bonnie to school where they hang out in the middle school media center. Visiting the rabbits has become as much a part of coming to the media center as checking out a book.

Photo by Mandy Sanders

Angel dressed up her Miniature Dachschunds, Princess Weiner-Fred and Prince William Williams, for a Valentine's Day picture. She then used the picture to create homemade Valentine's Day cards for her family and friends.

Photo by Angel Williams

Despite their different attitudes (Myles is a manly man, and Maggie is a girly girl), this Lhasa Apso and Shih Tzu are devoted to each other.

Photo by Alexa Helverson

The unusual and distinctive Chinese Shar-Pei arrived in the U.S. from Hong Kong in 1973, in an effort to save the breed. The dogs make wonderful pets for the right parents. Barbara, pet parent to Lucky and Cupcake, describes her dogs as loyal and loving.
Photo by Barbara Lee

Look at the heartwarming sisterly love between these two French Bulldogs, Pinky and Daisy.
Photo by Meishia Kernahan

Bailey, a Labrador Retriever, said, "Hey, I want in this picture," when Sarah tried to snap a picture of her daughter.

Photo by Sarah Kerner

This photo captures Ginger and Rojo's first meeting. Their pet parents are friends, and after they gave each other the once over, they also became pals.

Photo by N. Koffler

**Cousins Bailey and Tosca Rose enjoy a cold
February day in Wisconsin. They sport matching
purple fleece jackets to stay warm.**

Photo by Julie Coleman

The Comfort of a Best Friend

Brooke was diagnosed with cancer when she was 5 years old, and she had always wanted a dog very much. Her father said, "If my little girl wants a dog, she can have a dog!" So Brooke's parents purchased a Toy American Eskimo named Snowball and surprised Brooke when she came home from the hospital. She was beyond thrilled with her new friend!

The dog was perfect for the family. He was Brooke's best friend and constant companion and was game for anything Brooke wanted to do with him. He even let Brooke dress him up and take him for rides in her stroller, and he never once attempted to jump out of the stroller! Once Brooke put doll curlers in his hair and dressed him in baby clothes. Snowball was a patient and devoted friend, never objecting and always willing to play along. You can see the love and special connection they share in this photo.

When Brooke felt sick, Snowball was attentive and loving, lying next to her on the couch to let her know that he was there and would always be there. When Brooke passed away at age 7, Snowball was by her side right up to the end. Snowball continues to be an important part of the family, and Brooke's parents will always be grateful for the love he gave their little girl.

Photo and story by Darby Brion

Even though these two are siblings, big brother Yukon Cornelius and little brother Bumble both have their own distinct personalities.
Photo by Tricia Lee McNabb

Janet first got Buddy and then decided he needed a friend, so she got Weezer. Now the two Schnauzers are inseparable.
Photo by Janet Wallace

Teddy guards the family home while also enjoying the sunshine on the front porch; he was adopted from a shelter, so he values and cherishes his family and his home.

Photo by Jessica Dettling

Brothers Midas and Sparky were born from the same dog parents, but in litters one year apart. Even with the age difference, they're the closest of pals.

Photo by Joe Cardo

Jack, a Spitz/Collie/Retriever mix, had the following verse penned in honor of this photo:

Jack and Jill went to the park to swing
   and play and run
Jack wagged his tail to let Jill know
   that he was having fun
"Ruff!" said Jack, "Hooray!" said Jill
   as gleefully they swung.

Photo by Jillian Frame

Linus and Cinnamon, two ferrets, let their pet parent snap their picture before piling out of their bag to check out their surroundings.

Photo by Dawn Jaeckel

Judy is the pet parent of Rosie, Wiley, and Lucy; her best friend is the parent of Guinness and Murphy. Although the friends don't live close, they do vacation together and bring their pets, also best friends, along for the trip.

Photo by Judy Van Cleeff

It's bath day for these **Cavalier King Charles Spaniels, Beau and Casey.**

Photo by Eileen Bridge

This is the first moment that Max met his "sibling" Buco, a cat. Although they are peacefully observing each other here, it didn't take long for Max to get mobile enough to chase Buco and grab his tail.

Photo by Amy Hawthorne

Both thoroughbred ex-race horses, Bummer was purchased through an organization that focuses on finding homes for ex-race horses, and Bogie was bought from a race horse trainer. Although neither was particularly fast, as race horses go, they still enjoy racing each other in the pasture.

Photo by Susan Rogers

Who's the big, tough, active dog of these two siblings? Pet parent Kathy says Chewy is Mr. Tough Guy and much more active than his sister Nicki, a Jack Russell Terrier.

Photo by Kathy Tugwell

Alan met his wife when his Yellow Labrador, Summit, made friends with her dog, Shiloh, at a local dog park. Now they are one big, happy family.

Photo by Alan Levin

Belle, a Jack Russell Terrier, is enjoying some love and a little silliness with her "brother."

Photo by Shanna Withers

Louie, a Miniature Dachshund, is described as lively and adventurous by pet parent Shirleen.

Photo by Shirleen Jacobs

Anjelika lies on top of anything and everything. Here Cookie is Anjelika's personal bunny cushion.

Photo by George Black

Vinny and Baxter like to hog their pet parents' bed, although they don't mind making room for each other.
Photo by Sarah Smith

Sassy took a spot in the middle of the sink, and her sisters quickly piled in to share the fun.
Photo by Patricia Thorner

Here Comes Trouble

7

Sure, pets are lovable, sweet, and guileless . . . most of the time. But you can count on them to get into the teensiest bit of trouble every now and then. Or every day! Whether it's having an accident in the house or "accidentally" eating your couch or your favorite pair of shoes, those little rascals keep life interesting. They want *all* your attention, and they'll get it any way they can. Even after they've dug up your garden, it's hard to be mad when they give you that adoring, loving look, as if to say, "Me? Trouble?"

Sometimes you can see trouble coming just by looking at their faces; they have a hard time acting blameless, and you may feel like you know what your pet is thinking just by meeting her oh-so-innocent eyes. You may even say, "Don't even think about it!"

And, of course, they'll obey you . . . until they get a chance to wreak havoc again. Take a good look at your pet, and you might catch her in the act—or scheming about what to do next!

Wesley and Winston McDuff love to visit Mimi, their pet grandparent. All Cindi, their pet parent, needs to say is, "Want to go visit Mimi?" and they jump into her car.

Photo by Cindi Ramirez

A true Italian Greyhound, Alessa loves to eat tomatoes right off the vine.

Photo by Carrie Shaffer

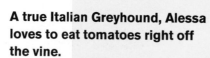

Pippen loves to hang out in high places and jump on her pet parents to wake them. Here she's found a perfect hiding/lounging spot under the Christmas tree branches.

Photo by Jeffrey Barber

Josie is hoping for a treat. No one would be able to resist those puppy eyes.

Photo by Jeanie Haas

Bruiser enjoys sipping soda, and he'll help himself to his pet parent's drink if he gets the chance.
Photo by Danielle Wells

Even though he can barely reach them and always gets splashed in the face, Billy, an English Bulldog, likes to drink from fountains.
Photo by Constantin Philippou

Barbara did some "fish sitting" for her grand-children's fish, and her cat, Spot, "helped." Red and Blue, the fish, did manage to survive all of Spot's attention.

Photo by Barbara Klokner

Priscilla Love, an English Bulldog, likes drinking from the faucet. She's getting ready for her bath in this picture.

Photo by Kelly Marascio

Described by his pet parent as rambunctious, Tucker relentlessly tries to get anyone in the house to play with him. His favorite games include fetch and tug of war.

Photo by Vickie Fan

Donning a Hawaiian shirt and glasses, Einstein, who lives on the Island of Maui, is ready for a trip to the beach.

Photo by Sally Goodness

All the kids had goggles on the first trip to a Florida beach, so Annie Fannie, a Boxer, also wanted a pair.
Photo by Jennifer Murnane

Harry, a Himalayan, likes to hang out in the window blinds.
Photo by Eileen Shin

Mischief and Miles

An English Bulldog, Miles has a great capacity for love . . . and mischief. His seemingly calculated transgressions require an infinite amount of patience by his pet parent, Heather. She tries to see the "talent" in his mayhem.

Take, for instance, his affinity for fine footwear. Heather claims that when making his selection of shoes to dismantle, Miles is particularly adept at discerning the most expensive ones. He also has potent powers of foresight. If Heather needs a particular supportive undergarment to match an outfit she plans to wear, Miles invariably seeks it out and renders it decidedly unsupportive.

Whether or not the object in question is truly edible rarely deters him. He has eaten rocks, sticks, leaves, bamboo furniture, wicker, fabric, string, wood, and other unknown items. And while he has gotten sick from his unique eating habits, it's never been too serious. Miles even once managed to expel the heel of Heather's favorite shoe!

After each episode, though, Miles gives Heather a look that she claims asks, "Can you really be mad at this face?" And she caves, unable to resist her charismatic, sweet, spoiled, loving dog.

Photo and story by Heather Hafer

Sweetie Pooh loves to climb up on the bird bath and admire his reflection in the water. His pet parent, Phyllis, wonders whether he's saying, "Mirror, mirror in the bath, who's the fairest of all the cats?"

Photo by Phyllis Perry

Mario and Marcie appear to be just taking a little lie-down, but they might actually be conspiring about their next endeavor.

Photo by Zan Farr

Tinker Bell was found wandering on a residential street close to downtown San Jose, California. The Wildlife Center gave Dina a call, and she added "Tink" to her family of three other goats.

Photo by Dina Hawkins

It was a hot day, so Genevieve found a cool spot to sit, relax, and watch as her pet parent cleaned out the refrigerator.

Photo by Diane Boeck

Maddie waves hello from behind her puppy gate. From the start, she's been a big ball of playful energy.
Photo by Karen Fairchild

Merlin, always the gentleman, enjoys a bit of tea and conversation with his pet parent's granddaughter.
Photo by Helen Doyle

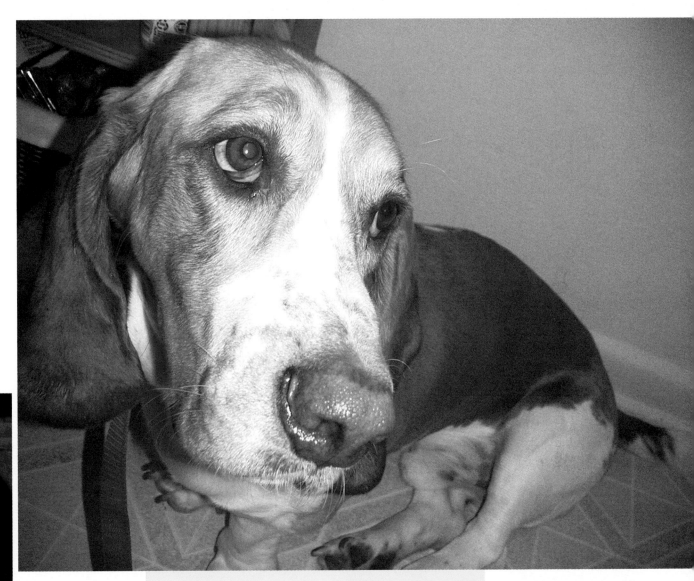

Banana is sweet and lovable, but causes trouble if left alone for 5 minutes. Pet parent Kirstin, however, says it's impossible to stay mad at him when he flashes his apologetic look, as here.

Photo by Kirstin Nes-ladicola

Sushi doesn't look very thrilled after her bath, but the soak is a tiny bit of payback for all the times the cat has hidden, jumped out, and scared her pet parents.

Photo by Luke Arrington

Christopher was once a content slacker, but his life changed when he adopted Molly from a rescue shelter. Now he finds himself walking several miles every day, standing outside at a dog park in freezing weather, reading and researching dog issues (especially animal rescue organizations), and loving every minute of it.

Photo by Christopher Spilker

Although he had to have his front leg amputated after he was hit by a car, Nico wasn't slowed by the accident. After the operation, he ran down the hallway, jumped on his pet parent, and was ready to play.

Photo by Regina Musso

While small in size, Peanut's appetite is big—and so is his bone!

Photo by Peggy Northrop

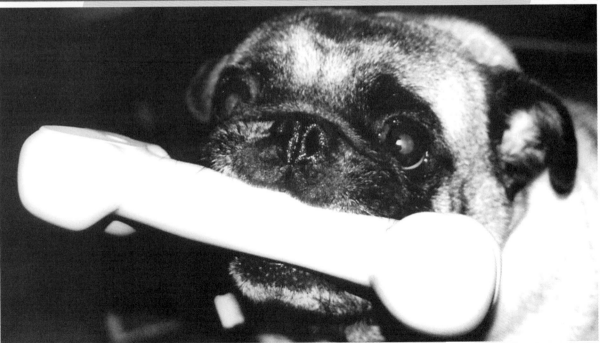

Dashiell (a.k.a., Dash) got caught here about to cause some trouble!
Photo by Melissa Denick

Is it trouble for Max, a Havanese? Or is he really trying to potty-train himself, as his pet parent suggests?
Photo by Ginger Leppert

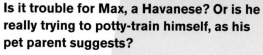

Who are you calling little? Bloomer has big ideas as he tries to drag this shoe around.

Photo by Amy Stevens

Flash's pet parent claims he loves to read, especially craft books. Note the book on upholstering next to his current DIY project.

Photo by Sue Cone

Haley likes to know what's going on around her, including what's going on outside the window.

Photo by Rosanne Haut

The kitchen counter is the perfect spot for Jasper to recline and keep an eye on things.

Photo by Michelle Bristow

8

That's Incredible

All a pet has to do to knock our socks off at the end of a rough day is be willing to snuggle close while we watch TV or go for a brisk walk around the neighborhood. Their ability to calm us, invigorate us, bring out our love is innate, and they'd be amazing and an important part of our lives if all they did was greet us at the door or give us an encouraging glance.

But they can do so much more. Our pets are not only our buddies, but they can be astonishing athletes, detectives, fearless acrobats, and sympathetic therapists. Some can perform camera-worthy tricks without flinching. Some participate in charity events. Many have important jobs and take their roles seriously, giving 110% every day. Whether it's running an agility course or searching for victims of a national tragedy, our pets are truly incredible.

Pets bring so much to the lives of their families and everyone around them, and they continue to astonish us every day with their talent and their willingness to share it. Regardless of the skill, all pets are deserving champions in our eyes.

From his humble beginnings as an abandoned dog, Shiloh has, with his adoptive pet parent's help, become a search-and-rescue dog. Shiloh completed more than two years of rigorous training and testing and has responded to nearly a dozen missing-person searches in Maryland, Virginia, Pennsylvania, and West Virginia.

Photo by Ed Mitchell

Starting at 4 months old, Barkley showed an interest in jumping. He participates in Dock Dogs competitions and has won several ribbons.

Photo by Janice Zelinka

Albert does his best trick, hoping to get a treat.

Photo by Jenny Ogg

Although he lost the use of his hind legs due to degenerative myelopathy, Schafer never lost his spirit and continues to enjoy playing, with help from his cart.

Photo by Pamela Marin

Tuesdays with Shadow

Jill found Shadow at a local Humane Society. Soon after she brought Shadow home, Jill saw an ad that called for sweet, loving, good-natured dogs to work with the elderly or sick. She thought Shadow fit the bill perfectly and immediately enrolled her in the therapy-training session.

After Shadow completed her training, Jill looked for a place they could visit regularly. As a special education teacher, Jill decided to take Shadow to work with her special-needs students. Thus "Tuesdays with Shadow" began.

Every Tuesday, Shadow comes to "work," where she helps students with their social skills, responsibilities, and speaking abilities. Each week, several students have alone time with Shadow, and they read to her, teach her new vocabulary words, work on math, and enjoy the dog's love and attention.

Now Jill is known at school as "Shadow's mom," and the students greet her and Shadow with joy. She is so proud of her little pound puppy and the impact Shadow has had on the lives of some very special students.

*Photo and story by
Jill Rosenthal*

Nap is quite a tightrope walker, sashaying on this very narrow railing.
Photo by Robert Grayson

Danica found her dog Carter through the ACES English Setter Rescue. He's completed obedience training and is currently working on his therapy dog certification. Because the dog is deaf, Danica and Carter communicate with hand signals.
Photo by Danica Barreau

Ever since he was a puppy, Marley and his pet parent have been training in search and rescue. Marley, a Labrador Retriever, is certified in wilderness, disaster, cadaver, and water searching.

Photo by Sandra Peavey

Gidget was rescued from an animal shelter and now enjoys running agility courses.

Photo by Amy Carlton

Diagnosed with neurological damage due to distemper, Boo's front legs were crossed at the ankles, and he was unable to separate them. When he walked, he put his crossed legs in front and then hopped forward with his two hind legs, often landing on his chin. With love, patience, massage therapy, and even acupuncture from his pet parent and her friends, Boo's legs did separate, and now he can move them independently.

Photo by Penelope Starr

One of Mele's favorite tricks is to balance a tennis ball on her nose and then quickly turn her head and catch it in midair.

Photo by Carol Islam